PRAYING WITH THE PSALMS

Cardinal Gianfranco Ravasi

Preface by Pope Francis

NOTES ON PRAYER

Volume 2

Our Sunday Visitor
Huntington, Indiana

Our Sunday Visitor Publishing Division
Our Sunday Visitor, Inc.
200 Noll Plaza
Huntington, IN 46750
1-800-348-2440

ISBN: 978-1-63966-270-8 (Inventory No. T2937)
eISBN: 978-1-63966-271-5
LCCN: 2024948707

Cover and interior design: Amanda Falk
Cover art: Adobestock

Printed in the United States of America

Contents

Preface by Pope Francis

Prayer is the breath of faith, its most proper expression. It's like a silent cry that comes out from the heart of whoever trusts and believes in God. It's not easy to find words to express this mystery. How many definitions of prayer we can gather from the saints and masters of spirituality, as well as from the reflections of theologians! Nevertheless, it is always and only in the simplicity of those who live prayer that prayer finds expression. The Lord, moreover, warned us that, when we pray, we must not waste words, deluding ourselves that thus we will be heard. He taught us rather to prefer silence and to entrust ourselves to the Father, who knows the kind of things we need even before we ask for them (see Mt 6:7–8).

The Ordinary Jubilee of 2025 is already at the door. How to prepare ourselves for this event, so important for the life of the Church, if not by means of prayer? The year 2023 was set aside for a rediscovery of the conciliar teachings, contained especially in the four constitutions of the Second Vatican Council. It is a way of keeping alive the mandate that the Fathers gathered at the council wished to place in our hands, so that by means of its implementation, the Church might recover its youthful face and proclaim, in a language adapted to the men and women of our time, the beauty of the Faith.

Now is the time to prepare for a year that will be dedicated entirely to prayer. In our own time the need is being felt more and more strongly for a true spirituality capable of responding to the great questions which confront us every day of our lives, questions caused by a global scenario that is far from serene. The ecological-economic-social crisis aggravated by the recent pandemic; wars, especially the one in Ukraine, which sow death, destruction, and poverty; the culture of indifference and waste that tends to stifle aspirations for peace and solidarity and keeps God at the margins of personal and social life. … These phenomena combine to bring about a ponderous atmosphere that holds many people back from living with joy and serenity. What we need, therefore, is that our prayer should rise up with greater insistence to the Father so that he will listen to the voice of those who turn to him, confident of being heard.

This year dedicated to prayer is in no way intended to affect the initiatives which every particular Church considers it must plan for in its own daily pastoral commitment. On the contrary, it aims to recall the foundation on which the various pastoral plans should be developed and find consistency. This is a time when, as individuals or communities, we can rediscover the joy of praying in a variety of forms and expressions. A time of consequence enabling us to increase the certainty of our faith and trust in the intercession of the Virgin Mary and the saints. In short, a year in which we can have the experience almost of a "school of prayer," without taking anything for granted (or at cut-rate), especially with regard to our way of praying, but making our own, every day, the words of the disciples when they asked Jesus: "Lord, teach us to pray" (Lk 11:1).

In this year we are invited to become more humble and to leave space for the prayer that flows from the Holy Spirit. It is he who knows how to put into our hearts and onto our lips the right words so that we will be heard by the Father. Prayer in the Holy Spirit is what unites us with Jesus and allows us to adhere to the will of the Father. The Spirit is the interior Teacher who indicates the way to follow. Thanks to him the prayer of even just one person can become the prayer of the entire Church, and vice versa. There is nothing like prayer according to the Spirit to make Christians feel united as the one family of God. It is God who knows how to recognize everyone's needs and how to make those needs become the invocation and intercession of all.

I am certain that bishops, priests, deacons, and catechists will find more effective ways this year of placing prayer as the basis of the announcement of hope which the 2025 Jubilee intends to make resonate in this troubled time. For this reason, the contribution of consecrated persons will be of great value, particularly communities of contemplative life. I hope that in all the shrines of the world, privileged places for prayer, initiatives should be increased so that every pilgrim can find an oasis of serenity and return with a heart filled with consolation. May prayer, both personal and communal, be unceasing, without interruption, according to the will of the Lord Jesus (see Lk 18:1), so that the kingdom of God may spread, and the Gospel reach every person seeking love and forgiveness.

As an aid for this Year of Prayer, some short texts have been produced which, with their simple language, will make possible entry into the various dimensions of prayer. I thank the authors for their contribution and willingly place into your hands these "notes" so that everyone can rediscover the beauty of trusting in the Lord with humility and joy. And don't forget to pray also for me.

Vatican City
September 27, 2023

Franciscus

Introduction

_____

The sound of the trumpet rang out through the streets of the cities and villages, its echo spreading across the countryside: it was the signal of the fiftieth year, proclaiming "liberty throughout the land to all its inhabitants." This act, as found in the book of the priests of ancient Israel, in Leviticus 25, marked the year of jubilee, named after that trumpet, in Hebrew *jobel*. Also in Christianity, in different forms and at different times, similar events have taken place, and we too are now heading toward the Jubilee of 2025. For biblical Israel it was a time in which the inhabitants and the land rested, refraining from any agricultural activity, eating of the spontaneous gifts of nature. The rest that we now experience with the Holy Year has another dimension: it is an intense time, dense with spirituality. Filled with two fundamental acts.

The first is that of prayer and meditation. The great seventeenth-century French thinker and believer Blaise Pascal cautioned:

The ancient philosophers said, "Go back within yourselves! That is where you will find your peace." But this is not true. Others say, "Go out! Seek happiness in amusements." But this is not true. Happiness is neither outside of us nor inside of us. It is in God, and then it will be outside and inside of us. (*Thoughts*, no. 391)

Here, then, is the meaning of the pages of this volume: it is an invitation to enter the Jubilee Year holding in one's hands the Psalter, which is the quintessential book of the Bible meant for prayerful pause and contemplative silence. It is a guide to "singing to God with art" through the Psalms. As St. Augustine said, "the great work of men is to praise God" (*Magnum opus hominum laudare Deum*).

But there is a second act that blossoms from prayer and makes this holy time a "year of the Lord's favor." Already in ancient Israel it was the time for setting slaves free. This is what Jesus was suggesting in His sermon in the synagogue of His village of Nazareth, quoting the prophet Isaiah. Prayer, singing, the liturgy do not close us off within a sacred oasis amid incense, candles and rituals, but beckon us to go out into the community and history. Here, in fact, are the words of Christ: "The Spirit of the Lord is upon me, because he has anointed me to proclaim good news to the poor. He has sent me to proclaim liberty to the captives and recovering of sight to the blind, to set at liberty those who are oppressed, to proclaim the year of the Lord's favor" (Lk 4:18–19; Is 61:1–2).

It is the commitment to keep our steps far from the paths of evil, aggression, hatred and injustice, to make firm the path of love and solidarity that leads us to recognize the face of Christ in our suffering and marginalized brothers and sisters. In fact, as will be seen, the Psalms do not drive the worshiper to take flight from everyday reality toward heavens of fantasy or of vague mysticism, but to travel the roads of history, including the rocky ones, and to live the faith in the day of celebration but also in the dark night of trial. The Psalter throws its songs open wide to the hubbub of social existence, to the works and days, to the laughter and tears, to the personal dramas and national tragedies. Always, however, with one certainty: even if "father and mother have forsaken me, / but the Lord will take me in" (Ps 27:10).

This little guide to the Psalms includes four cardinal points: a general reflection on prayer, the breath of the soul; a panoramic look at the psalmic texts; a portrait of the two protagonists, God and the worshiper, but also the intrusion of the presence of evil; and finally, an anthology of brief commentaries on the Psalms most dear to tradition and the liturgy. The hope is that all the faithful may draw fully from this "wonderful treasury of prayers," as the Second Vatican Council called the Psalter (see *Dei Verbum*, 15).

Prayer, Breath of the Soul

———

"The ancients rightly said that praying is breathing. Here one sees how foolish it is to want to talk about a 'why.' Why do I breathe? Because otherwise I would die. So it is with prayer." In his diary, the nineteenth-century Danish philosopher Søren Kierkegaard jotted down these words, developing a symbol dear to the spiritual tradition: prayer is a bit like the oxygen that allows the soul to breathe, and if the sacraments are akin to the food of the spirit, there is no doubt that the breathing of prayer precedes and accompanies the entire religious experience. For this reason, according to the tradition of Judaism, prayer is the "great reward of human existence."

The joyful song of praise
The Psalms are par excellence the prayer of Israel and of the Church, and yet in them all of creation is caught up in the praise of God, from the animals to the stars in the sky. Before we set off along the paths

of this biblical book, we would like to cast a glance at an immense horizon that spans our entire planet and extends across the centuries. It is the world of prayer in its thousand forms according to the different religions, and unexpectedly sometimes even among the nonbelievers who raise to heaven, for them bereft of divinity, a cry or an invocation.

This is how, for example, a twentieth-century Russian atheist writer prayed. Aleksandr Zinoviev said:

> I beg you, my God, try to exist at least a little, for me. You need do nothing but follow what happens: it's so little! But, O Lord, take the trouble to look: living without witnesses is hell. Therefore, straining my voice, I cry out: My Father, I beg you, exist!

For believers, however, prayer is much more and is, as we have said, necessary in order to live spiritually and even physically.

Let us content ourselves, in this panoramic view, with remarking the appearance almost of two regions with antithetical colors. Along these expanses run different pathways of prayer. The first is — if we wished to adopt a chromatic image — the "red" one, bright, warm, festive and harmonious. It is the song of *praise*. It is the glorification, worship, grateful acknowledgment, celebration, contemplation of God and His works. He is exalted not to obtain a particular gift, but for the simple fact that

He exists and reveals himself in words and actions. The most common literary expression of this is the *hymn*, which is present in all of humanity's religions and has a significant place, as we will see, in the Psalter.

The synthesis of this form is the "alleluia," which in Hebrew means precisely "praise the Lord": it adorns some of the psalms and also belongs to our joyful liturgy. It is a song that expands into a blessing: "Bless the LORD, O my soul, / and all within me, / bless his holy name" (103:1). Or it becomes thanksgiving for His salvation and is a yearning of the soul: "O God, you are my God; earnestly I seek you; / my soul thirsts for you" (63:1). Perhaps the emblem of the highest Christian praise is in the song *Gloria in excelsis*, or in the prayer of Jesus: "I thank you, Father, Lord of heaven and earth, that you have hidden these things from the wise and understanding and revealed them to little children" (Mt 11:25).

The bitter supplication

There is, however, another region of prayer into which we must enter, and it is, to use the chromatic metaphor again, the "violet" one, the other extreme of the color spectrum, with a colder dimension, marked by pain, by tears, by the empty silence of a God who seems absent but to whom one cries out. It is the *supplication* or lamentation that often unfolds according to a formula that is also documented in the Psalms: the bitter present is contrasted with the past, along with a hoped-for liberation in the future. The "I" of the worshiper is contrasted with an evil "other," not rarely personified in enemies, and at the end comes the invocation of the triumphant coming of a supreme "Other," the savior God.

The adversary, however, is sometimes not outside of us in hostility, in illness, in trial, but is inside, in our very soul and life. And it is sin. One then raises prayers to God for forgiveness, confesses one's sins, recognizes God's justice and entrusts oneself to His merciful goodness. Everyone knows the spiritual and poetic power of Psalm 51, called the *Miserere* after the first word in its Latin liturgical version. So supplication has different nuances, and Jesus himself urged us to use it as a key to open the door of God's heart: "Ask, and it will be given to you; seek, and you will find; knock, and it will be opened to you," because "whatever you ask the Father in my name, he may give it to you" (Mt 7:7; Jn 15:16).

The distinctive Christian prayer, the "Our Father," admirably summarizes these two colors of prayer. The first three invocations, in fact, are the quintessential praise of God, His person (the "name"), the kingdom of love and justice that He wants to establish in history, His salvific will. The other four petitions are, instead, a supplication for daily bread, the forgiveness of sins, liberation from temptations and evil. The intertwining of praise and supplication then permits the comprehension of another fundamental dimension of prayer.

It is what St. Paul essentially formulates when he writes to the Christians of Rome, "I appeal to you therefore, brothers, by the mercies of God, to present your bodies as a living sacrifice, holy and acceptable to God, which is your spiritual worship" (Rom 12:1). For the Semitic world, the body is not a reality opposed to the soul, but is the unitary expression of the person. This is why the Jewish worshiper, rocking his body in prayer, moves all its joints so that his whole being may take part in praying. This is why the prophets fought against worship that was inward-focused and alienated from life. Amos puts it bluntly:

I hate, I despise your feasts,
    and I take no delight in your solemn assemblies.
Even though you offer me your burnt offerings
        and grain offerings,
    I will not accept them …
Take away from me the noise of your songs;
    to the melody of your harps I will not listen.
But let justice roll down like waters,
    and righteousness like an ever-flowing stream.
                                (Amos 5:21–24)

Jesus himself was clear in uniting prayer and life, liturgy and charity: "Not every one who says to me, 'Lord, Lord,' will enter the kingdom of heaven, but the one who does the will of my Father" (Mt 7:21), and "so if you are offering your gift at the altar, and there remember that your brother has something against you, leave your gift there before the altar and go. First be reconciled to your brother, and then come and offer your gift" (Mt 5:23–24).

Prayer is not a magical act, but a choice that echoes throughout all of existence, just as the liturgy must not be restricted to the sacred oasis of Temple ritual amid songs and incense, but must radiate into the square, that is, into everyday life, into social commitments, into the contradictions of life, into decisions between good and evil, right and wrong, true and false.

Praying with the Psalms

_____

Psalterium meum, gaudium meum! "O my Psalter, my joy!": so exclaimed St. Augustine in commenting on Psalm 138. This biblical book — which is made up of 19,351 Hebrew words in the original (it is the third by length, after the texts of Jeremiah and Genesis) — with its 150 songs has been for centuries "the voice of the bride [the Church] addressed to her bridegroom," as Vatican II stated in its document on the liturgy (*Sacrosanctum Concilium*, 84), continuing the tradition of the Temple of Jerusalem and the Jewish synagogue. Evocative and significant are the titles that tradition has given to this prayerful poetic collection: in Hebrew, *Tehillîm*, that is, the "praises," the celebration of the Lord by His faithful; in Greek, *Psalmoi*, with allusion to the musical dimension of the performance, whence the Latin *Psalterium* and our Psalter and Book of Psalms.

The palace of the Psalter
The aim of this presentation is not to go into the complex historical-critical questions connected to the

formation of the various compositions and the subsequent redaction in a single work, nor to delve into the exegetical analysis of each individual ode. Although tradition attributes them to King David, the Psalms are an expression of the age-old faith of the people of God in various eras of its history. For this reason St. Jerome, the translator of the Bible into Latin, provided a vivid image in comparing the Psalter to a palace that requires two sets of keys for access: the great key of the entry gate, that is, the Holy Spirit who inspired it, and a series of specific keys for each individual room, namely for each psalm.

We will content ourselves with offering a basic overall guide: this will be like standing on Mount Nebo, contemplating the Promised Land in the same way Moses did. Ours will be, therefore, first and foremost a panoramic look at the general thematic characteristics of the whole collection of the Psalms, in order to make possible their recovery and re-actualization in the prayer and life of the Christian, especially at an intense and powerful time like that of Jubilee. This fulfills what a Jewish mystical author of the last century, Abraham J. Heschel, used to say: "A song every day, a song for every day."

Before beginning this portrait of the Psalter, let us remember just one marginal external fact that is, however, necessary for the use of the individual psalms: it is the question of their numbering. We adopt, as in current Bibles, the Hebrew calculation which, starting from Psalm 10, is generally of greater unity than that of the Latin translation (the latter is still in use today in the liturgy). The variation is due to the fact that two Psalms, 9 and 10, were merged into a single Psalm, 9, in the Greek and Latin versions of the Psalter. But now let us turn our gaze to these prayerful songs, to their different tones, to their themes and to the multiple literary genres that they reveal.

The faces of the Psalter

The Psalms are, fundamentally, poems full of colorful and exotic Oriental language, full of symbols and linked to their own literary forms. Significant, for example, is what is referred to as *parallelism*, whereby a concept is reiterated two or three times in different but similar forms. Moreover, the psalmic images rise up to the heavens where the Lord reigns, "wrapped in light as with a garment," and descend to *Sheol*, in Hebrew the land of the dead, the underworld, the Abyss, populated by ghosts and plunged in silence. The eye of the psalmists turns to the imposing cedars of Lebanon, which soar high into the ever clear sky of the Orient, but also rests on the hyssop, a slender plant that grows between the stones of the walls. The whole Promised Land is drawn with all its geographical and social landscapes: from the most terrible, the hurricane, which shakes the forests (cf. Ps 29), to the desert lands, to the animals and to national historical events, up to the delightful picture of a mother with her child in her arms (Ps 131), as we will have occasion to illustrate.

The Psalms are poems to be sung to musical accompaniment in the liturgy; they are choral prayers to be performed along the lines of melodies already known at the time, as is often indicated in the titles placed at the opening of many compositions of the Psalter. Thus, to the soloist who sings the song of the gifts that God has sown in the history of Israel, the liturgical assembly is to respond with the repetition of the antiphon "his mercy endures for ever" (Ps 136). The Temple and community worship are the heart of the book of Psalms, which thus also becomes a text of prayer that is official for Israel and "ecclesial" for Christianity.

The Jews divided the Psalter into five "books" or collections (Ps 1–41, 42–72, 73–89, 90–106, 107–150): in this way the five great "words" spoken by God in the *Torah*, the first five books of the Bible (Genesis, Exodus, Leviticus, Numbers and Deuteronomy), are accompanied by the five "words" of response of faithful Israel. Thus the dialogue between God and man is born. The word of God and the word of man meet, the former becoming incarnate, the latter becoming divinized.

The Psalms, then, throw themselves wide open to human existence, to mourning and celebration, to politics and intimate affections; the noise of the streets and cities fades, but it does not disappear as if we had come to a silent hermitage where all is still and all is forgotten. These texts, which embrace a span of almost a thousand years of Israel's history, are a model not only of prayer, but also of life. In this regard, we can cite a well-known comparison from the Jewish tradition. A leaf held up to the light reveals a network of veins that feed and support the connective tissue of which it is composed; in the same way, the Psalms innervate life without negating it in its concrete realism, but supporting and nourishing it. The mysticism that arises from this is not hazy and generically spiritual, but has zest, blood, body, just like the person who lives in everyday life.

The Psalms are, therefore, the mirror of those who with sincere hearts seek God within their history. The Creed of Israel too is a sequence not of abstract articles of faith, but of actions that God has carried out over the centuries on behalf of His people (cf. Dt 26:5–9; Jos 24:2–13; Ps 136). The most complete formula of faith and the highest form of prayer in the Bible are in recognizing, professing and meditating on the great works of God (Ps 78, 105, 106). The itineraries of prayer that the Psalms offer are therefore linked to the human journey, to our times and to those stretches of human history which we must travel and in which we must discover the presence of God-Emmanuel. Let us try, then, to follow their main trails.

The rainbow of psalmic prayer

The French poet Paul Claudel depicted the succession of prayers in the Psalter using the image of the colors of the rainbow: the 150 odes that make up the book of Psalms truly represent a rainbow of problems, joys, hopes, sadnesses, bitternesses and multiple states of mind. Let us try to identify the most striking colors that are expressed through a few of the forms or models that scholars call "literary genres."

1. The crisis. In the Psalms the color of suffering dominates, certainly more than that of joy: almost a third of the Psalter is marked by lamentation and pain, just like the life that knows more darkness than happiness. Grave illnesses, national tragedies, implacable enemies create around us a wall of coldness, hatred and even violence and persecution (for example, Ps 7:2; 35:19; 38:20; 69:5; 86:14, 17; 142:7). It is what the Bible calls "the enemy" and constitutes, with the worshiper and with God, the three characters of the drama that every supplication contains.

Sometimes this antagonist is even more dangerous, because it is lodged inside the man who prays: it is his sin, which makes him experience the tragedy of God's silence (Ps 38, 51, 130).

Other times, as in Psalm 73, it is the crisis of faith that the believer experiences in an anguished way, when he sees "there is a righteous man who perishes in his righteousness, and there is a wicked man who prolongs his life in his evildoing" (Eccl 7:15). The scandal of injustice and innocent suffering brings to the lips of the worshiper the eternal demand that seems to fade into a question: "How long, O LORD, will you look on?" (Ps

35:17). In suffering, prayer takes on an audacity and immediacy like that of the piercing cry of Job (ch. 3) or Jeremiah (20:7ff.). The first word of these psalms is precisely the anguished invocation of the name of the Lord (for example, Ps 3:2; 6:2; 7:2).

But one certainty always emerges in psalmic prayer: the mute and distant God, who even seemed indifferent, intervenes in the end by granting the supplication. The Bible does not know total and suicidal desperation: the finale of all the psalms of lamentation is always projected toward a future of liberation (the sole exception is perhaps Psalm 88, to which we will refer later). It is, therefore, necessary to immediately line up another color, after the gloomy one of supplication.

2. Hope, trust, and thanksgiving. Psalmic prayer is, in fact, permeated by a luminous current of hope and trust that arises precisely from the biblical concept of faith. To believe, as in the original meaning of the Hebrew word for faith, the root of our *amen*, is to rest upon a stable rock that does not admit of collapse: it is to build upon God, the "hope of Israel" (Jer 14:8), and not upon the sands of doubt. In fact, "It is better to take refuge in the Lord / than to trust in princes" (Ps 118:8). The believer goes through the dark tunnel of crisis and pain with the certainty that it does not lead to nothingness, but to peace and joy.

The image of the flock entrusted to the sure guidance of the shepherd, its travel companion (cf. Ps 23) under the relentless sun of the desert and along the desolate tracks of the steppe, and that already mentioned of the "weaned child with its mother" (Ps 131:2) are the symbols of this attitude of prayer (cf. Ps 4, 11, 16, 27, 46, 62, 115, 125, 129, 131). In fact, "In you our fathers trusted; / they trusted, and you delivered them. / To you they cried and were rescued; / in you they trusted and were not put to shame." (Ps 22:5–6).

Hope sustains not only the short span of a trial or an earthly event, but, little by little, pervades the entire parabola of human existence up to the hard-fought passage of death, which is no longer annihilation and darkness, but "the path of life, / in your presence there is fullness of joy, / at your right hand are pleasures forevermore" (Ps 16:11; cf. Ps 49 and 73). It is the theme of eternal communion with God, which has already blossomed in fidelity to His word during earthly existence.

This trust, a specific theme of some psalms, also enlivens and makes possible the communal and personal thanksgiving that forms the basis of a series of psalms (9–10, 30, 32, 34, 65–68, 92, 116, 118, 124, 138). It may be surprising that compared with the vast litany of laments in the Psalter, the joy of gratitude should be so scarce and expressed in a tone less intense. Of course, since the Bible also bears witness to man and his reality, this imbalance reflects a sad and unfortunately constant experience. Gratitude faces a steeper path in people's minds than does asking for favors. Of the ten lepers healed, only one returned, "praising God with a loud voice; and

26

he fell on his face at Jesus' feet, giving him thanks" (Lk 17:15–16).

But neither must one forget, as has been said, that biblical supplication indeed concludes with the anticipation of thanksgiving, in fact with the confident certainty that happiness is just around the corner, because "will not God give justice to his elect, who cry to him day and night? Will he delay long over them?" (Lk 18:7). The last word that the faithful one offers to the Lord is always of peace and serenity, because he knows that his cry of pain falls not into nothingness but upon a transcendent ear: "I thank you that you have answered me, / and have become my salvation" (Ps 118:21).

3. *The prayer of worship and enthusiasm.* This is the model of prayer in its pure state: it is the spontaneous and free praise of God, which we have already had occasion to outline on a general level. It is what the exegetes call a *hymn*: there is no longer a concrete motivation to prompt the prayer as in the psalms of thanksgiving, no more reference to a specific gift that has been obtained. God is thanked for the sole fact that He is present, lives, works and communicates; He is contemplated in His eternal and continuous love; He is celebrated for His great glory that He displays first and foremost in nature.

Thus were born the *hymns to the Creator*: often these are dominated by wonder at the grandeur and splendor that envelops all cosmic reality, and sometimes the focus is brought to bear on the most fascinating temporal being in the universe, "little lower than the angels"

(Ps 8:6): man. Among these hymns, mention should be made of this same Psalm 8, a song of the greatness of the human person; of what is called the "psalm of seven thunders," the 29th, the setting of which is a storm and which some scholars consider one of the oldest texts of the Psalter, based on themes from the surrounding world, archaic yet enduring and effective for Israel too; of Psalm 103 or 104, which perhaps retains an echo of the Egyptian hymn to the sun composed by the "monotheistic" pharaoh Amenhotep IV.

Other compositions celebrate the presence of God in the history that He leads toward the final kingdom established by His Christ: they are the *hymns of the kingdom of God*, marked by the enthusiastic acclamation "The LORD reigns" (Ps 93:1; 96:10; 97:1; 99:1). The kingdom of God is recognized as eternal (Ps 93), universal (Ps 94:2; 96:10). Therefore, "Let the be glad, and let the earth rejoice; / let the sea roar, and all that fills it; / let the field exult." The Lord, "will judge the world in righteousness / and the peoples in his faithfulness" (cf. Ps 96:11–13).

Finally, another center of praise is *Zion*, the pole of attraction of every Jewish heart (Ps 46, 48, 76, 84, 87, 122). The hill on which the Temple stands is the point of confluence of the living streams of pilgrimages that the Jews and all of humanity undertake, eager to find peace in Jerusalem ("He makes wars cease to the end of the earth; / he breaks the bow and shatters the spear / he burns the chariots with fire" [Ps 46:9; cf. Is 2:1–5].)

As soon as "the holy habitation of the Most High" (Ps 46:4) appears before the pilgrim's astonished eyes, hope is reborn, because "the Lord of hosts is with us" (v. 11). In fact, "the LORD loves the gates of Zion / more than all the dwellings places of Jacob" (Ps 87:2).

In the hymn the whole human person, with his emotions, his expectations, his frailty and his greatness, is called to a grandiose celebration that is joyfully expressed in the refrain of the *alleluia* or the antiphon "his love endures for ever," which — as we have already seen — punctuates all of Psalm 136. The entire existence of man in fact becomes a "living sacrifice, holy and acceptable to God" (Rom 12:1). In the Christian rereading, man seeks, in the prayer of praise and adoration, to model himself ever more on Christ, who says to the Father, "I glorified you on earth, having accomplished the work that you gave me to do." (Jn 17:4).

4. *Liturgical prayer.* The hill of Zion, seat of the Temple, is always a point of reference and attraction for the Jewish believer: "I was glad when they said to me, 'Let us go to the house of the LORD!'" (Ps 122:1). "Even the sparrow finds a home, / and the swallow a nest for herself / where she may lay her young, / at your altars, O LORD of hosts, / my King and my God" (Ps 84:3). If the liturgy in the Temple is the highest synthesis of all of Israel's social and personal life, it may come as a surprise that so few fragments of liturgical rituals should be preserved in the Psalter. But we must not forget that many psalmic compositions have ritual at their origins,

and that the entire collection of the Psalms would go on to constitute the foundation of Jewish and Christian worship.

It is natural, then, that prayer with the Psalms should also flow into the liturgy today and find its most intense expression there. No individual ever prays alone to the exclusion of the community, but is always a member of the chosen people that dialogues with the God of the covenant and of the election of all Israel. The halo of the pact and of the "holy nation" surrounds every worshiper who lifts up his voice to the Lord.

In particular, two psalms, 15 and 24 — which are almost to be equated with the penitential acts prior to the Christian celebration of the Word and the Eucharist — present us with the authentic attitude with which to approach the liturgy. If this is not to be reduced to farce or magic, it must take root in life, in our relationships with God and neighbor in justice, love and faithfulness, as reiterated at length in the central message of many of the prophets (cf. Is 1:10–20; Am 5:21–24; Hos 6:6; Mic 6:6–8; Jer 6:20). The Decalogue, with its religious and community requirements, thus becomes the essential touchstone of the genuineness of our celebrations and ceremonies (cf. also Ps 50, 52, 53, 75, 81, 95).

Worship must not be a pretext for shirking the commitments of interior and social faithfulness, spirituality and solidarity: this is not enough when justice toward one's neighbor is lacking. "O LORD, who shall sojourn in your tent? / Who should dwell on your holy hill? /

He who walks blamelessly and does what is right, / and speaks truth in his heart" (Ps 15:1–2). "For you will not delight in sacrifice, or I would give it; / you will not be pleased with a burnt offering. / The sacrifices of God are a broken spirit; / a broken and contrite heart, O God, you will not despise" (Ps 51:16–17). The exemplary commentary on these Psalms is to be found in the voice of the prophet Micah: "'With what shall I come before the Lord, / and bow myself before God on high? / Shall I come before him with burnt offerings, / with calves a year old? / Will the Lord be pleased with thousands of rams, / with ten thousands of rivers of oil?" And, "He has told you, O man, what is good; / and what does the Lord require of you / but to do justice, and to love kindness, / and to walk humbly with your God?" (cf. Mi 6:6–8).

5. *Prayer and political and cultural life.* If echoes of political events and national catastrophes are not lacking in the Psalms (for example, Psalm 78, or the "collective supplications," such as Psalm 44), it is above all the figure of the sovereign, descendant of David that is the focus of attention for a series of compositions probably intended for the liturgy of the enthronement and coronation of the king (Ps 2, 18, 20, 21, 72, 89, 101, 110, 132).

But the admittedly lively interest that the Jew feels for his history, also witnessed to by the historical psalms (Ps 78, 105, 106, 111, 114, 135, 136), goes beyond the simple desire to compile the annals of the Jewish state or to leave a picture of the political, social and economic

31

events in which Israel was involved. The figures, often dull and sinful, who succeed one another on the political stage through the Davidic dynasty are the sign of a more decisive presence of God, who, precisely through these frail and imperfect instruments, continues to lead salvation history toward more exhilarating aims. The "consecrated" (in Hebrew "messiah") who now sits on the throne of David is destined, albeit within the limits of his weakness and unfaithfulness, to offer the proclamation and hope of the advent of the definitive "consecrated/messiah," "son of God" (cf. Ps 2:7) as the Jewish sovereign in a higher sense. This will be the full and perfect meaning that the royal psalms will acquire in the rereading that Christianity carries out in the light of the figure of Christ.

In prayer, the believer's social experience is also illuminated, while maintaining its autonomy, reality and specific characteristics. The man who encounters God is not a disembodied being, but a creature placed on the earth "to work it and keep it" (Gn 2:15). He therefore comes to God with his knowledge and intelligence. It is what the Bible calls *wisdom*, a human quality that embraces all sectors of formation: social themes (justice, prudence, mercy, instruction), ethical themes (commandments, relationships with others), philosophical problems (retribution according to one's works, the suffering of the innocent and the related theodicy, that is, the justification of God despite the existence of evil) and religious (theology and mysticism).

These are what are called the "wisdom psalms," which apply human experience, intellectual reflection, learning and thoughts that assist in the understanding of reality, to probe certain questions of communal life and personal affairs (Ps 90, 37, 49, 73). Or these psalms become catechesis — that is, a theological exploration of God's will: This is the case of the monumental Psalm 119, dedicated to the celebration of the Law as divine word. *Torah*/Law has in Hebrew a much broader meaning than our own because, as has been said, it certainly embraces the whole Pentateuch, that is, the first five books of the Bible, but on a more general level it is the revelation of the word of God and the expression of Israel's response. Psalm 119 delves precisely into the divine Law in all its dimensions, in all its values and in all its requirements, as indicated by a sample of terms used by the psalm itself to define this (order, commandment, statute, precept, way, word, instruction, testimony …).

6. *The imprecatory psalms.* Embedded in the Psalter are some compositions that have often caused a scandalized reaction in the Christian community, so much so that they have been expunged from current liturgical use. These are what are called the "imprecatory psalms," whose fabric of invectives embarrasses the disciple of Christ, who is instead supposed to love his enemy and forgive him, even if unfortunately history overflows with quite different examples. They are the expression of an ancient and distant culture and social atmosphere, and so must be interpreted correctly, certainly not in a

literal sense, considering the fact that the law of retaliation in reality aims to respond to the needs of distributive and retributive justice, so as to match every crime with an equal or identical punishment and practically eliminate the evil.

But now we will try to explain the rationale of these pages, which are still under the seal of divine inspiration. First of all, these words are animated by the same indignation as that of the prophets in the face of the brutal and bloody manifestations of evil in human history. They reveal an ardent anxiety for justice, they become a prayer made of flesh and blood, ready to involve the whole being of the person, body and feelings, passion and reason. Jesus himself sometimes manifests this indignation against hypocrisy and injustice, brandishing the whip against the merchants of the temple (cf. Jn 2:13–22) or hurling genuine curses and invectives, as can be read in chapter 23 of Matthew.

Moreover, one characteristic of Semitic symbolic culture is that the use of abstract concepts is alien to it: evil, therefore, is often personified in a concrete enemy. And Oriental language loves strong images, strong verbal expressions, the bright warmth of words. Such truculent tones are strikingly represented in these lines of Psalm 58 hurled against the powerful and against corrupt politicians: "O God, break the teeth in their mouths; / tear out the fangs of the young lions, O Lord! / Let them vanish like water that runs away. ... Let them be like the snail that dissolves into slime, / like the stillborn child that never sees the sun. ... The righteous will rejoice when he sees the vengeance; he will bathe his feet in the blood of the wicked. Mankind will say: 'Surely there is a reward for the righteous; surely there is a God who judges on earth'" (Ps 58:7–12).

The fierce rhetoric, the violence of the tirade, the trust of Semitic culture in the efficacy of the word when it blesses and curses, are part of the social psychology underlying these imprecations, but they also indirectly reveal the underlying moral anxiety, so much so that the final exclamation refers to trust in a God who brings justice on earth, and vengeance is entrusted to Him alone. St. John Chrysostom, a fourth-century Father of the Eastern Church, saw in these invectives a living sign of the "abasement" of God, who "adopts language, human conceptions and truths yet imperfect." It is the theme of the correct interpretation of the sacred violence present in the Holy Scriptures (holy war, tribal conflicts, martial symbols applied to God): it belongs to the historicity of biblical Revelation.

The word of God is not a series of perfect and abstract theological theorems: it is indeed a truth, but one that makes its way through human events with all their weight of evil, blood, misery, pain, and not only with their light, beauty and love. It is, in practice, an application of the Incarnation that brings the *Logos*, the divine and transcendent Word, into the living and often dramatic "flesh" of human history (Jn 1:14). This divine presence must reckon with the reality of the freedom of the person, which is not erased and overwhelmed by God. He in fact wanted His creature to be free for good or for ill, and therefore inclined not only to obey but also to violate His laws (Gn 2–3).

And yet the goal to which He wants to lead history and human choices themselves is a horizon of light where "death, mourning, crying, pain" cease (cf. Rv 21:4). For this reason St. Paul, quoting a passage from Deuteronomy (32:35), exhorts Christians: "Beloved, never avenge yourselves, but leave it to the wrath of God; for it is written, 'Vengeance is mine, I will repay, says the Lord.'" (Rom 12:19). And he continues, referring to a passage from the Book of Proverbs (25:21): "'If your enemy is hungry, feed him; if he is thirsty, give him something to drink; for by so doing you will heap burning coals on his head.' Do not be overcome by evil, but overcome evil with good" (vv. 20–21).

The Psalms, Word of God
and of Humanity

———

"It is at first very surprising that there is a prayerbook in the Bible. The Holy Scripture is the Word of God to us. But prayers are the words of men. How do prayers then get into the Bible? … Thus if the Bible also contains a prayerbook, we learn from this that not only that Word which he has to say to us belongs to the Word of God, but also that word which he wants to hear from us" (Dietrich Bonhoeffer, James H. Burtness (tr.), *Psalms: the Prayer Book of the Bible*, Augsburg Publishing House, Minneapolis 1970, pp. 13, 15). This significant observation comes from Dietrich Bonhoeffer, the theologian and martyr of Nazism in 1945, in the brief volume he dedicated to praying the Psalms.

The encounter between God and the worshiper
Biblical Revelation is, in fact, dialogic: The Word of God is interwoven with the human word, and their encounter is placed under the seal of inspiration. It is therefore natural that the Psalms should be a manifestation of this embrace between God and the worshiper, who

are the two protagonists. They are bound together by a relationship of love and faithfulness, expressed above all with the Hebrew term *hesed,* which resonates a hundred times in the Psalter and which generates an intimacy between God and His faithful. This is the reason for the frequent echoing of possessive adjectives and personal pronouns: "my/our" as addressed to God occurs 75 times; about fifty times Israel is called "his" people; ten times "his" inheritance and seven times "his" flock.

It is an interpersonal relationship that is also defined through mutual "remembering." On one side, there is the Lord who remembers His faithful, the people He has chosen and taken to himself through a covenant to which He always remains faithful (Ps 105:8) and which He implements with His actions in salvation history (Ps 78: 4–5). On the other side is the worshiper's "remembering," a verb that becomes a sort of synonym for "believing." In fact, the Psalms make frequent appeals to "remember God" (Ps 77:3), to "remember your wonders of old" (77:11), to "remember your name" (119:55).

As a result the relationship with God takes on a tone of communion, of mystical intimacy, described through a variegated symbolism that we leave to the reader of the Psalter to discover, especially when he uses it as a book of prayer: the table, the cup of wine, the perfume intended for the guest, satiety, being quenched, dwelling together on the holy mountain of the Temple, the parched earth fertilized by rain, the shadow that gives refuge from the heat of the sun, the wings that protect, the intimate warmth of the nest, mutual desire and so on.

In this encounter a special significance is taken on by the symbol of *light*, which, moreover, is a sign of the divine mystery used by all civilizations: "For it is you who light my lamp; / the LORD my God lightens my darkness" (Ps 18:29). The Word of God is "a lamp to my feet, / and a light to my path." (Ps 119:105). The human person certainly proceeds with the guidance of reason and the senses, but the divine word is dazzling and, like the sun, makes other lamps pale. Now, the symbol of light encloses precisely the link between divine transcendence and human historical reality. In fact it is, like God, outside of us, entirely superior; it precedes us and exceeds us; it cannot be grasped with the hands and subdued. Yet it envelops us, penetrates and warms us, specifies us, identifies us, enlivens us.

Creature and Creator encounter each other in the halo of light which thus becomes a sign of revelation. Exemplary in this sense is Psalm 19, which we will have occasion to present in the final anthology: it intertwines the two lights, that of the sun which speaks of its Creator and reveals Him to us in creation, and that of the Law, the *Torah*, the commandments of the Lord, which are "pure, / enlightening the eyes," so that "by them is your servant warned" (cf. Ps 19:9,12). Along these lines it becomes clear how significant it is to "see God" and His face, hence in the Psalter we often come across the expression "let thy face shine" (Ps 80:3,

19; 119:135).

Obviously at the opposite extreme is God's "hiding His face," which generates this repeated invocation in the Psalms: "Hide not your face from me. / Turn not your servant away in anger" (27:9). If the radiant face of the Lord is the source of life, joy and hope, its darkening or removal or "turning away" becomes the root of judgment and anguish: "Hide not your face from your servant, / for I am in distress; make haste to answer me" (69:17). A corollary to this symbolic constellation of light and face are the verbs of "vision," which likewise presuppose a meeting of gazes between God and the worshiper. The series of psalmic texts that extol this crossing of the divine and human eye is very rich.

Here are just a few examples. On God's part: "The LORD's throne is in heaven; his eyes see, his eyelids test the children of man" (11:4). "[The LORD] looked down from his holy height; / from heaven the LORD looked at the earth, / to hear the groans of the prisoner, / to set free those were doomed to die" (102:20–21). "The eyes of the LORD are toward the righteous" (34:16). "Precious in the sight of the LORD / is the death of his saints" (116:15). On the worshiper's: "My eyes are ever toward the LORD" (25:15). "My eyes are grow dim / with waiting for my God" (69:3). "To you I lift up my eyes, / O you who are enthroned in the heavens! / Behold, as the eyes of servants / look to the hand of their master, / as the eyes of a maidservant / to the hand of her mistress, / so our eyes look to the LORD our God, / till he has mercy upon us" (123:1–2). Indeed, all creatures and all living things have the same attitude: "The eyes of all look to you, / and you give them their food in due season" (145:15).

We could conclude at this point with a tender appeal that exalts the divine and human value of this symbol: "Keep me as the apple of your eye" (17:8). Vision and contemplation are the harbor of prayer: here is the seal of the encounter between the two protagonists of the Psalter, the Lord and the worshiper, God and the human self in an embrace and dialogue of love, even in the time of trial and darkness. And it is precisely in this latter situation that a third subject wedges itself in, appearing to shatter that bond between the two protagonists of the Psalter and to break off the words and gazes.

The third presence

This is a negative figure that assails the harmony between God and His creatures. In biblical language, it is "the enemy," which, as we have already had occasion to say when speaking of prayer in its general and universal form, is a typical presence in supplications, that is, in invocations against the evil that besets the faithful. Of course, in some cases this could be a personal adversary who undermines the worshiper, who slanders him, humiliates him, persecutes him. The portrait of betrayal in Psalm 55 is original and evocative: "For it is not an enemy who taunts me — / then I could bear it; / it is not an adversary who deals insolently with me — / then I could hide from him. / But it is you, a man, my equal, / my companion, my familiar friend. / We used to take sweet counsel together; / within God's how we walked together in the throng" (55:12–14).

Other times it can be the high-handedness of the powerful, or the hostile force of an army coming against the holy city, as in the case of the collapse of Jerusalem under the Babylonians in 586 BC (Ps 74:137). This is the dominant theme in the national psalmic lamentations (Ps 44, 79, 80). Often, however, the enemy becomes a concrete personification of evil, illness, unhappiness. In this case too there is recourse to various symbols that for now we can only list, leaving it to those who use the Psalter as constant reading and prayer material to discover them verse by verse. Thus, martial images are often on display: the sword, the bow, arrows, the shield, war, military defeat.

Sometimes the enemy/evil is instead embodied with symbols of hunting or the animal world: hunting with traps and nets, ferocious beasts such as lions, rabid dogs, raging bulls. One need only consider Psalm 22, which Jesus recited on the cross: "Many bulls encompass me, / strong bulls of Bashan surround me; they open wide their mouths at me, / like a ravening and roaring lion. / For dogs encompass me" (22:12–13, 16). And the invocation continues: "Save me from the mouth of the lions" (v. 21), specifying however that what surrounds the worshiper is "a company of evildoers" v. 16), so as to unravel the meaning of the bestial metaphor.

The reader will also come across symbols of nature in the pages of the Psalms, such as destructive flood waters that beset the believer up to the throat, or the risk of slipping into a deep pit that seems to plunge him into the underworld, or again the aridity of the soil that generates thirst. The evil that is introduced between God and the human creature can often be illness in all its varieties and symptoms, ranging from leprosy to loss of appetite and fever. But what stands out in particular is that sort of playground of Satan which is solitary isolation, abandonment, rejection by others.

But there are two more dark and disconcerting presences, able to create serious crisis in the dialogue between God and man. First of all is the *silence* of God himself, His detached remoteness as a sovereign impassive and indifferent to the suffering of His creatures. These are appeals as harrowing as those of Job, as in the famous opening of the aforementioned Psalm 22 used by Jesus on the cross: "My God, my God, why have you forsaken me? / Why are you so far from saving me, from my words of my groaning? / O my God, I cry by day, but you do not answer; / and by night, but I find no rest" (22:1–2). Indeed, that divine silence seems to be a sign of hostility, with the previously evoked image of "hiding the face" (a good 22 times in the Psalter), His "turning away" and even the "inflaming of His anger." This is the most arduous test for the faithful.

The other hostile presence is, instead, strictly human, and it is *sin*, which is a violation of morality and disobedience to the divine word. Famous in this regard are the previously cited psalms 51 (*Miserere*) and 130 (*De profundis*). It is only with the confession and repudiation of this enemy inherent in man himself that dialogue blossoms again through conversion, reconciliation and God's forgiveness, which is stronger than the sinner's offence. The lexicon that expresses the wiping away of evil in this case is evocative: the "not remembering" of guilt on the part of the Lord who again "turns His face" to the worshiper, who "covers" (*kipper*) the sin so as to wipe it away, but also man's *shûb*, literally his "return" to the right path after the deviation of sin, and therefore his "conversion." An admirable synthesis that describes the resumption of dialogue interrupted by human rebellion is found in Psalm 103, laden with mysticism: "For as the heavens are high above the earth, / so great is his steadfast love toward those who fear him; / as far as the east is from the west, / so far does he remove our transgressions from us" (103:11–12).

In conclusion, the Psalms are a prayer that engages God and humanity, eternity and everyday events. They are a call to walk in the light of the divine word, they are an entreaty to be saved from the evil outside and inside of us, they are a resolution to keep "my feet from every evil way, / in order to keep your word" (Ps 119:101). But the present of the Bible is always situated within a movement toward the future. Odysseus, torn from his country, longed to return to his lost homeland and his past, even just to contemplate the smoke rising from the chimneys of the houses (*Odyssey* 1, 58). His homeland was a "return," a "before." Abraham, the type of the biblical believer, is instead a pilgrim on the earth, because his homeland is an "after," an "onward."

The prayer of the Psalms helps us to seek out this future not by flinging ourselves from reality toward dreams or fantasies of escape, but by committing ourselves every day to our earthly journey, which has a luminous destination: "For you will not abandon my soul to Sheol, / or let your holy one see corruption. / You make known to me the path of life; / in your presence there is fullness of joy; / at your right hand are pleasures forevermore" (Ps 16:10–11).

Imitating Jesus, who at His last Passover sang the *Hallel*, the collection of Psalms intended for solemn liturgical celebrations (perhaps Ps 113–118 or Ps 136: see Mt 26:30), the Christian community — especially in the time of jubilee — through the Liturgy of the Hours and that of the Word joins this chorus that has been rising to God for centuries. St. Paul's appeal is significant in this regard: "Let the word of Christ dwell in you richly, teaching and admonishing one another in all wisdom, singing psalms and hymns and spiritual songs, with thankfulness in your hearts to God" (Col 3:16).

A Psalter in Miniature

So far we have adopted a sort of contemplation from above: we have, in fact, already used the image of the view from the summit of Mount Nebo when Moses, on the threshold of his death, had the panorama of the promised land before him, but also heard that cold prohibition of the Lord: "I have let you see it with your eyes, but you shall not go over there" (Dt 34:4). After the pages dedicated almost to describing the map of the Psalter in its characteristics and in the different colors of its literary and religious regions, we now — unlike Moses — would like to delve into some of those territories.

It is obviously not possible to propose a reading guide for all 150 psalms, considering the basic and limited nature of the resource presented here. So we decided to make a selection of the most significant psalmic songs, and those best known and of the widest liturgical or spiritual use, also capable of accounting for those "literary genres" described above (hymns of praise, supplications, professions of trust, thanksgivings, songs of Zion and the kingdom of God, wis-

dom compositions, meditations on salvation history
and so on). To each of the Psalms we will dedicate
only a minimal interpretation, a sort of spotlight that
will reveal the theme for further discovery and exploration in meditative reading at length. So now it is
essential to take the Bible in hand and open it to the
section dedicated to the Psalms, so as to be able read
the texts that will be presented in turn (the liturgical
numbering of the psalm is indicated in parentheses).

Psalm 1: The two ways

Opened in the original Hebrew by a word that begins
with the first letter of the alphabet, *alef,* this wisdom
composition is almost the key to understanding the
whole collection of the Psalms. Two ways, two destinies,
two humanities are set off against each other: The just
who sings the Psalms is like a leafy tree that does not see
its leaves wither; the unjust is dry like chaff scattered by
the wind. The last letter with which this Psalm ends is
tau, last in the Hebrew alphabet: the Psalm is, therefore,
a conceptual alphabet of morality and man's choices in
history.

―――≈◈◈◈≈―――

Psalm 2: The Messiah king

Here is one of the most famous pages of the Psalter:
with Psalm 110 it represents the classic messianic
prayer of Christianity. In itself, however, the ode is a

text of the solemn coronation liturgy of the king of Judah. On that day, according to an Oriental practice, a divine quality was assigned to him: "You are my Son. / Today I have begotten you" (v. 7). If for Israel the sovereign will remain only the Lord's adopted and not His natural son, in the Christian rereading the king-messiah of the psalm will be Christ, the Son par excellence. Noises of rebellions are heard in the background, but God takes the side of the "son" whose scepter will break all resistance of evil as if it were an earthenware jar. And all will prostrate themselves before him and "with trembling kiss his feet."

<hr />

Psalm 6: Heal me, Lord!

"I can't hold out any longer!": This is the dramatic plea of a sick person who feels in his physical decline the icy tentacles of Death. In the nebulous vision of the afterlife that Israel then had, the realm of the dead is a place of silence from which God is absent (v. 5). The intense demand for life that the sick person makes of God is, therefore, something more than a simple request for healing. It is the desire to rediscover life and intimacy with the God who now seems hostile: this is why the Christian tradition has set this psalm as the first of the seven penitential psalms (6, 32, 38, 51, 102, 130, 143). In this light suffering is interpreted as the fruit of sin, according to an ancient conception that linked suffering to guilt. But, as always in biblical supplications, the last word is one of hope and life: "for the LORD heeds the sound of my weeping" (v. 9).

———⁓⁓⁓———

Psalm 8: Little less than a god

Committed to the sands of the moon by astronauts Neil Armstrong and Edwin Aldrin at the invitation of St. Paul VI, this psalm is an extraordinary celebration of man in the grandiose fabric of the creatures of the universe. Yet, in the "eternal silence of infinite spaces," this "thinking reed" — to use the image of the famous seventeenth-century French philosopher Blaise Pascal — is a microscopic grain. Even more insignificant is his reality in the face of an all-powerful creator God who in the sky embroiders with His fingers the constellations and planets. Yet it is precisely this God who bends down to man and crowns him, making him little less than himself, the sovereign of the cosmic horizon. A song of humanism, therefore; a prayer that is risky when man becomes a tyrant and humiliates the world. This is why the Letter to the Hebrews turned this nocturnal psalm into the song of the perfect man, Christ (cf. 2:5–10).

———⁓⁓⁓———

Psalm 16 (15): The path of life beyond death

A stupendous composition, perhaps written by a priest:

the language of the divine "inheritance" present in vv. 5–6 is typical of the Levitical class, which did not have its own territory in Israel but lived around the Temple. The poetic and religious heart of the psalm is, then, in the profession of faith in v. 2: "You are my Lord; / I have no good apart from you." One seems already to hear the words of St. Teresa of Avila: "Whoever has God lacks nothing; God alone suffices." Heartened by this trust, the poet even dares to issue a challenge to man's supreme fear, that of death. On the one hand he sees his days relentlessly streaming toward the pit, but on the other he understands that the God of life cannot allow His faithful one to plunge into nothingness or into the ghostly abode of the dead. To his eyes there appears almost a glow: it is the path of life and eternal joy before the face of God. Peter, in his speech at Pentecost (cf. Acts 2:22–36), and Paul in his in Antioch of Pisidia (Acts 13:14–43) will repeat the words of Psalm 16, applying them to the risen Christ.

⸻ ⟨⟩ ⸻

Psalm 19 (18): The light of the sun and of the Word

Two suns, two lights, two divine words: the sun, light and word of creation, the secret voice of God; the sun, light and word of the *Torah*, in practice for the Bible the explicit voice of God. One famous medieval Jewish commentator wrote, "Just as the world does not come alight and live except by the action of the sun, so the soul does not reach its fullness of light and life except through the *Torah*." The sun is not a god like Ra or Aten, the Egyptian solar deities; it is just a splendid creature that, like a groom or an athlete, emerges from the bed of night to run along the orbit of the sky. And in its blaze it has a higher encrypted message to reveal, that of its Creator. The *Torah*, the Law of God, is instead the explicit, pure, radiant and eternal word of the Lord. Whoever welcomes it with joy tastes as it were honey with an inscrutable flavor, he possesses as it were an unparalleled treasure.

Psalm 22 (21): My God, why have you forsaken me?

There is no Christian who does not know the shocking force of this famous lamentation's opening lines, cried aloud by the dying Jesus (Mt 27:46). A text of great desolation, streaked with blood and tears, marked by "bestial" images of a purely Oriental flavor (bulls, lions, mastiffs, wild oxen), depicting in filigree a body with dislocated bones, a heart as soft as wax, with a throat like parched clay, with labored breathing, with wounded hands and feet. All around, the silence of God and the hostility of the men who are already dividing the inheritance among themselves, convinced that they have before them a man cursed (v. 18). And instead, suddenly, comes the turning point: "You have answered me!" (cf. 22:20–22). And the lament turns into a hymn of festive thanksgiving (vv. 23–27) and into a song to the Lord, king of the universe (vv. 28–29). From desperation to hope, from death to life, from the tomb to the resurrection (vv. 30-31).

―――⟨ຉຉ⟩―――

Psalm 23 (22): The Lord is my shepherd

"The hundreds of books I have read have not brought me as much light and comfort as these verses of Psalm 23." This testimony of the French philosopher Henri Bergson (1859–1941) clearly expresses the constant fascination exerted on readers by this lyric, studied, loved and continually echoing in Christian liturgies. There are two symbolic unities that undergird the poem: the first is the pastoral one, so dear to the biblical and Oriental tradition in general (Ez 34, Jn 10), the second is that of hospitality (the table, the perfumed oil, the filled cup), a sign of intimacy. The shepherd is not only the guide, he is also the travel companion, and so he shares the same hours as the flock, the same risks, the same thirst and hunger, the identical relentless heat. The meal of hospitality evokes, instead, the sacrifice of communion in the Temple, which included a sacred banquet with the meat of the immolated victim. The two symbols speak, therefore, of communion and intimacy between God and man: "For you are with me" (v. 4) is, then, the decisive word of the psalm, and trust is the underlying attitude.

—◈—

Psalm 29 (28): The seven thunders of a storm

According to many scholars, this dazzling storm chorale is one of the most ancient psalms: it takes words, symbols, ideas from the indigenous pre-Israelite world, that of the Canaanites. The ode is marked by a dark onomatopoeia: the Hebrew word *qôl*, which means both "thunder" and "voice," resounds seven times. In the unleashed cosmos the poet therefore glimpses a sign of the Creator. In Canaan the storm was seen as the orgasm of Baal, the god of rain and fertility. In the psalm, however, it is only an instrument with which God unveils His transcendence: He is above the storm, and in Him and with Him there is only peace (vv. 10–11). The storm is dramatized as it unfolds: from the Mediterranean to the mountain chain of Lebanon (Sirion is the Phoenician name), up to the southern steppes of Kadesh, where the pregnant deer and sheep abort due to the terror of the lightning and thunder. But in the cyclonic whirlpool of history and nature we have a fixed point in Him, the Lord who "blesses his people with peace."

—◈—

Psalm 39 (38): Man who lives is like a breath

This heartbreaking autobiographical elegy on the pain of living seems to have been written by a brother of Qoheleth, the famous pessimistic scholar of the Bible. In fact, three times there echoes to a crescendo the term *hebel,* dear to that author (Eccl 1:2; 12:8): often translated as "vanity," it actually means breath, impalpable sough of wind, elusive shadow, cloud that dissolves at the first appearance of the sun. This is also how life is for our poet, an empty sequence of days, only as long as a span (v. 5), pervaded by the mania of possessing riches which are then corroded by woodworms. This great poet makes a single stark prayer: he cries out to God to grant him just a moment of peace, to let him breathe for just an instant, literally to let him swallow his saliva, as the colorful original phrase in verse 13 intended to indicate a moment of respite. And then, in the still obscure Old Testament view of the afterlife, there will be only the emptiness of *Sheol,* the underworld of the Bible.

Psalms 42-43 (41-42): As the doe pants for water

The *Sicut cervus* by Pierluigi da Palestrina, one of the masterpieces of Renaissance music, could act as the backdrop to this wonderful lyric poem mistakenly divided into two psalms, 42 and 43, which is actually a single piece, as attested by the antiphonal refrain of 42:5, 11 and 43:4. It unfolds as the three-act auto-biographical story of a Levite who may have been "excommunicated" from Jerusalem and relegated to forced domicile in a foreign land, in upper Galilee, at the sources of the Jordan near Mount Hermon and Mount Mizar (precise location unknown). Even surrounded by the clear and cool waters of the holy river, he thirsts for another water, that of Zion. He is like the doe that, having reached a dry stream, raises its lament to the sky: the psalmist's throat thirsts for the living God who reveals himself in Zion in all His splendor. His nostalgia for the liturgy of the Temple (v. 4) is poignant, especially now that his enemies, the pagans, mock the righteous man by asking him, "Where is your God?" (v. 10). Unforgettable is the poet's soliloquy with his soul, present in verses 5 and 11, a call to hope, because God will not be silent to the end.

This is the third part of the single lyric made up of Psalms 42–43, mistakenly divided into two psalms. The Levite relegated to upper Galilee trustingly awaits the intervention of God, who will send his two messengers, Truth and Light (43:3). These will take the exiled worshiper by the hand and bring him to Zion, to the altar of God where the believer will resume his liturgical service with singing and dancing. In crescendo, the antiphon that had already been sung twice in Psalm 42 (vv. 5, 11) resonates for the last time (v. 5): now his words are about to come true because

God, after the test, will show himself as "the salvation of my countenance," that is, as joy and as light. One passage from Psalm 43 has been used by Christian tradition as the entrance prayer for the Eucharistic liturgy according to the ancient Latin rite: "*Introibo ad altare Dei* … I will go up to the altar of God."

⸻

Psalm 49 (48): Riches and death

This "oratorio on death" is another of the literary and spiritual masterpieces of the Psalter. A grand wisdom meditation on the true scale of human values, the prayerful song strives to rend the dark veil of death, the final frontier of earthly existence, to discover its mystery. The voracity of the monster called *Sheol* (as we know, the underworld of the Bible) swallows up riches and goods: in vain does the powerful delude himself that with his immense finances he can offer a ransom to Death. No matter how high the sum offered, it will never be enough (v. 8). And while knowing this truth, the rich man is like a beast already marked with the seal of the end, who deludes himself that he can win and survive: he — as the antiphon of verses 12 and 20 literally says — "does not make it through the night" and it is immediately the end, he "does not understand" his fate, bestially obtuse as he is.

But for the righteous a light is kindled in the darkness of death. The eternal God, Lord of life, cannot let those who have lived with Him in the intimacy of love and justice plunge into nothingness. And this is the poet's testament: "God will ransom my soul from the power of Sheol; for he will receive me" (v. 15).

———

Psalm 51 (50): *Miserere!*

The *Miserere* is, perhaps, the most famous psalm, meditated upon, interpreted, set to music, even painted (by the French artist Georges Rouault) by an immense group of repentant and converted men. The poetic and spiritual core of this supplication is, in fact, entirely in that passionate "Against you, you only, have I sinned" (v. 4). Jewish tradition, precisely on the basis of this confession, has attributed the psalm to David, adulterer with Bathsheba and murderer of her husband, Uriah (2 Sm 10–12). In reality the style, the prophetic theme of the "spirit" and the "heart" as the perfect sacrifice (v. 19), the plea for the rebuilding of the walls of Jerusalem after the Babylonian exile of the 6th century (v. 20), suggest a later era. Nonetheless, the inner power of this prayer remains intact, which is like a terrain half covered with darkness (the dark region of sin in vv. 3–11) and the other half with light (the luminous region of grace in vv. 12–19). But if the sense of guilt is keen, more intense is the experience of forgiveness, of newness of spirit, of the joy that the Merciful God pours out upon the repentant sinner. So more than a penitential song, Psalm 51 is the celebration of the resurrection to life in the spirit of the evangelical parable of the prodigal son, or better, of the merciful father (Lk 15:11–32).

Psalm 63 (62): My soul thirsts for you

A psalm much loved by the mystical tradition for the thirst and hunger for God that pervades it, this lyric is also a masterpiece of symbolic compactness, despite the changing tones, from supplication to hymn. From the thread of the physical symbolism a true geography of the soul is woven: it thirsts for the infinite like the arid, thirsty ground, cracked by the heat; it is hungry for the meat of the sacrifices (v. 6), that is, for worship; its lips await the honey of praise. The goal is that of a much dreamed-of embrace, after a night of vigil and waiting: "My soul clings fast to you" (v. 8). But this song of total intimacy with God ends on a dark scene, populated by jackals, swords, dark and infernal places, liars. It is, however, the proclamation of the end of evil: in the mystical bond one discovers an irrepressible optimism toward history.

Psalm 72 (71): The Messiah, king of justice

With Psalms 2, 89 and 110, Psalm 72 constitutes the

classic tetralogy of the royal psalms reread in a messianic key by the Jewish and Christian tradition. Behind the face of the young king who is about to be crowned, who is wished a reign of justice and long years, there is outlined the face of the perfect king, the supreme "consecrated/messiah" who will truly be a just judge for the poor and will truly "crush the oppressor" (v. 4). It is precisely in this long and glorious prospect that the laudatory tones of monarchical hymnology are turned into the hoped-for reality with the advent of the Messiah: his justice will be perfect, his dominion universal, his kingdom eternal, the entire cosmos will be caught up in peace, that is, in the awaited *shalôm* that verse 16 paints with the agricultural colors of an earthly paradise (the ears of wheat will sway even on the arid mountain peaks). The hymn, with a very refined structure marked by royal acclamations (vv. 5, 11, 17), closes with a supplemental blessing (vv. 18–19). This was added by the Jewish liturgical tradition, which had divided the Psalter into five books: the second book, which began with Psalm 42, ended here, with this blessing.

Psalm 73 (72): Beyond the crisis of faith

This extraordinary story of a soul records the inner travail of a believer, perhaps a priest, in a crisis of faith over the triumph of injustice in the world. His spiritual story becomes prayer, poetry and testimony through the two acts in which this wisdom meditation is arranged. The first, in verses 1–14, is the paired portrait of the wicked and the righteous as it presents itself in the scandal of history: the unjust is portrayed with a disdain and nausea difficult to overcome; the arrogance and vulgarity of power have here their most sarcastic representation. But the temptation to abandon all honesty and be like them is immediately broken off with an "until ..." (v. 17) which marks the transition to the second act. The poet, in fact, goes back into the Temple and into the silence of his conscience: there he manages to understand the fate, the "end," the "after" of the wicked and the righteous (vv. 17–28). Then his eyes are opened and in what has been called "the most beautiful spiritual text of the Old Testament" the psalmist leaves his final testament of faith and of hope: "For me it is good to be near God" (v. 28). And God takes him by the hand; even if his flesh and heart fail, the believer is welcomed into the arms of the Eternal. Here is another page of the Old Testament in which the horizon beyond death is lit up with light and certainty. "There is nothing on earth that I desire besides you" (v. 25).

―――≈∾∾―――

Psalm 84 (83): The song of the pilgrims

Opening with the astonished exclamation of a pilgrim come before the Temple, this poignantly beautiful canticle of Zion describes the longing of this same pilgrim as he is about to leave the holy city. In fact, the desire that pervades him during prayer passes through three tonalities. There is the ancient desire, rekindled during the journey through the Valley of Tears (a location variously identified), going from fortress to fortress as the first autumn rains begin to fall (v. 7). There is the desire satisfied in front of the Temple, in the intimacy of prayer, in the courts bustling with the celebration of the liturgy. Finally, there is the desire that is reborn when, before returning home, the pilgrim bids farewell and casts one last look upon Zion. It seems almost natural for him to envy the swallow and the sparrow that have their nests under the eaves and cornices of the Temple. Because being in Zion is like being in paradise, in the joy of intimacy with God. The palaces of the powerful or the pagan shrines may be fascinating, but the poet has already made, without hesitation, his choice: "For a day in your courts is better than a thousand elsewhere" (v. 10).

―――∽⁄∂⁄∂⁄∂∼―――

Psalm 87 (86); No one is a foreigner

This brief song of Zion is laden with an ecumenism that can be interpreted in various ways. Zion, in any case, appears as the root of cosmic cohesion, it is the source of all harmony for the layout of the earth and of the nations whose four cardinal points are clearly delineated: Babylon is the eastern superpower, Rahab, meaning Egypt, is the western, Tyre and Philistia represent the north, while Ethiopia represents the deep south. Well, in God's book of history all these peoples are registered as citizens of Jerusalem. Three times, in verses 4, 5 and 6, the Hebrew verb *jullad*, "he was born there," is repeated: all the peoples of the earth, no longer considered impure and pagan, have their maternal origin, their "springs" precisely in Zion, where the Lord dwells, the city that makes all men equal and at peace. For the Christian there is a natural reference to the Jerusalem of Pentecost in which all the nations hear proclaimed in their own languages the same "mighty works of God" (Acts 2:5–12).

Psalm 88 (87): The most anguished supplication

"The gloomiest psalm of the Psalter, the darkest of all the lamentations, the most dramatic *De profundis*, the Song of Songs of pessimism": these and other definitions coined by exegetes express the impression one gets in reading this extreme supplication flung to God as the feet of the worshiper seem to sink irreparably into the tomb and the horizon has become dark and silent. The intense cry, like an SOS fired off to God, develops two themes, the tomb (vv. 3–7) and complete solitude (vv. 8–18). *Sheol,* the biblical underworld, dominates the whole lamentation with its grim presence; it almost seems like a song of death that with its icy hand gropes over the bones and flesh of the worshiper. Death, however, is preceded by loneliness: the marginalized and alone, even if he is alive, is as if a corpse. Job too in very bitter pages lamented this silence of men (19:13ff.). But there is a further silence, that of God. If in the underworld the Shades keep quiet and God is mute toward them, the present silence of God is the sign that He has abandoned this man, sad since childhood, unhappy and sick (v. 15). And so the end has truly come: on the horizon there is not even a glimmer of light as in the other psalmic supplications. The only friend now is the eternal infernal darkness (v. 18).

Psalm 90 (89): Our years, like a breath

The fragrant and melancholy central image comparing men to the grass, which sprouts in the morning and in the evening is mowed down and withered, employs a theme dear to all of literature. In the *Purgatory*, Dante writes, "Your reputation is the color of grass / Which comes and goes, and that discolors it / By which it issues green from out the earth" (Dante Alighieri, Henry Wadsworth Longfellow (tr.), *Purgatorio*, George Routledge & Sons, London 1867, p. 284). This gentle but intense elegy on human transience has recourse to temporal images (a thousand years/one day, years/

days, morning/evening), spatial images (the dual movement of man's "return" to the dust and of God toward man) and psychological images (God's anger and mercy, man's anxiety and expectation) to express two sentiments. One side is dominated by the evil of living (vv. 1–10): our years are wispy and fragile like a sigh, but they are drenched with pain and trouble. The destination is made of dust, of shadow, of silence. But from the other side comes a plea for God to deliver us from this evil, to teach us to count our days that we may obtain wisdom of heart. By clinging with trust to the Lord, who is eternal, man who is vain and unsteady participates in an indestructible solidity, his works take on a new stability and their own permanence (vv. 11–17). A subtle hope of eternity therefore closes this elegy, which opened on emptiness and dust.

Psalm 92 (91): The song of the elder

Used in synagogue worship for the celebration of the sabbath, the great weekly feast, Psalm 92 indeed seems to be a hymn with a liturgical backdrop in which God is praised with songs and music for His love and faithfulness (vv. 1–3). The song is given over to a comparison between the righteous and the wicked before God (vv. 6–15). The portrait of the wicked is conveyed with the vegetal image, already known from Psalm 90, of the grass that sprouts up but is soon pulverized and destroyed for ever. Another vegetal image is used for the portrait of the righteous, but its tenor is quite different. Unlike the wicked, who is like the lush but ephemeral grass of the fields, the righteous rises toward the sky, solid and majestic like the palm tree and the cedar of Lebanon. His foliage spreads out into the celestial sanctuary and his roots sink into the holy and fruitful soil of the Temple: his canopy aspires to the infinite, his trunk is anchored in the eternal, his existence reaches the divine (vv. 12–14). Strength like that of the unicorn, beauty like that of a hero daubed with oil (v. 10), life like that of a majestic and age-old tree, perpetual fruits in perpetual youth: this is the enthusiastic song of the righteous that Psalm 92 contains in its verses.

———※———

Psalm 98 (97): The Lord, king of the earth

Lo and behold, a "new song," perfect and glorious, to the Lord as king and judge, whose seven fundamental qualities are called wonder, victory, salvation, justice, love, faithfulness, righteousness. But the song comes from an extraordinary choir and orchestra (vv. 4–8). It is not only the faithful who, accompanied by the instruments of worship in the Temple (harps, trumpets, lyres), acclaim the King and Lord. All creatures take part in the chorus: the roaring sea, the mainland with all its inhabitants, the rivers which with their branching streams seem like clapping hands, while the echoes of the valleys and mountains give forth deep and sustained sounds. The Lord's entry into the world and into history causes a shudder of happiness in everyone and everything. The world sings because God is in the midst of His creatures and is not expelled from humanity with the rebellion of pride and injustice.

—◦◦◦—

Psalm 103 (102): God, tender as a father

The "God is love" of the First Letter of John (4:8) seems almost preannounced in this blessing, which certainly extols divine justice but is open to forgiveness. Comprised of two blessings, the first personal (vv. 1–2) and the second choral/cosmic (vv. 20–22), the psalm develops along two movements. The first is a gentle song of love and forgiveness (vv. 3–9), a forgiveness that goes beyond the rigid laws of justice (v. 10). The second lyrical movement celebrates the relationship between divine love and human frailty (vv. 11–18), and does so through five highly effective similes: the vertical distance between heaven and earth, the horizontal distance between east and west, paternal tenderness, grass, and the flower of the field blasted by the burning desert wind. Towering over the whole scene is the loving goodness of God, expressed in part with an evocative Hebrew root that literally indicates the maternal "viscerality" of God's love for His creature. Weak and insubstantial man, "is few of days and full of trouble" (Job 14:1), is enveloped in the mercy of the LORD, which is "everlasting" (v. 17).

───⟨∘/∘/∘⟩───

Psalm 104 (103): Canticle of the creatures

According to some scholars, this splendid canticle of the Creator and of creatures bears a resemblance to the *Hymn to Aten* of the famous pharaoh Akhenaten (14th century BC), who had reformed Egyptian religion on the basis of a certain solar monotheism (Aten was the solar disk). What is certain is that our poet's perspective is different, because the sun is not divine but is only one of the many signs of God's splendor in the cosmos. Fascinated by the wonders sown throughout creation, the poet begins with the sky, lit up by a grandiose divine epiphany (vv. 1–4), contemplates the earth and the waters in tension (vv. 5–9), moves on to the countless manifestations of life, generated by water on the earth, germinated in animal and vegetable forms, bursting forth in the satiety of creatures (vv. 10–18). Next comes the mystery of time marked by the sun and the moon, by the nocturnal life of beasts and the diurnal life of man (vv. 19–23). The sea is no longer the chaotic monster that tries to demolish creation, but teems with ships and fish among which even the aquatic monster Leviathan dances, now reduced to a friendly whale (vv. 25–26). Over everything extends the creative spirit of God, who gives life its fullness and who, from the heights of His heaven, contemplates His masterpiece full of joy (vv. 27–34). And that all may sing praise to the Lord it is necessary for the world to be freed and purified from all profaners and all the wicked (v. 35).

Psalm 110 (109): The Messiah, king and priest

In the original Hebrew it is made up of only 63 words, yet this royal psalm has been one of the most studied, set to music and beloved of the Psalter. The classic messianic text since the time of Judaism, its words, not always clear in the original Hebrew, have been translated, elaborated and applied to the perfect king, heir to the priesthood of Melchizedek, the sovereign/priest of Salem, the pre-Israelite Jerusalem (Gn 14). The ode is structured on two parallel oracles. The first (vv. 1–3) is the solemn one meant for the sovereign on the day of his enthronement "at the right" of the ark, sign of the presence of God. The second oracle (vv. 4–7) is, instead, more of the priestly type, since in ancient times the king also played a ceremonial role, and it ends with a bloody vision of the triumphant king who smashes the skulls of his enemies, like the pharaoh in Egyptian depictions, and drinks from the streams on his military marches (vv. 6–7). In the ancient Greek version verse 3 became the proclamation of the divine filiation of the Davidic sovereign: "From the bosom of the dawn, like the dew I have begotten you" (cf. Ps 2:7). In this light the psalm has become a classic of Christology, as attested by numerous New Testament quotations (for example, Mk 12:36; Heb 1:3, 13, 7; Acts 2:34–35).

———

Psalm 117 (116): An ejaculatory prayer

Like a miniature, this mini-hymn, the shortest of the Psalter, made into music of ineffable beauty by Wolfgang A. Mozart in his *Solemn Vespers for a Confessor* (1780), has been used by tradition as if it were an ejaculatory prayer and a *Gloria* to be placed at the end of other songs or psalms. Its 17 words, only 9 of which are of import, are in fact the celebration of the heart of biblical faith, the covenant that God establishes with man through His love and faithfulness, in Hebrew *hesed* and *emet*. The poet enrolls in this praise all peoples, all songs of the earth, which are addressed to God, the great ally of humanity.

———

Psalm 119 (118): Imposing song of the divine word

This monumental alphabet of the word of God so eminently expressed by the Torah, the biblical Law, is like an Oriental song that unspools its melodic phrases in circles that spiral up into the sky in infinite repetitions.

This sort of "perpetual motion" of faithfulness to the divine word, a lamp for the steps (v. 105), sweeter than honey (v. 103) and more precious than fine gold (v. 127), is striking for its sophisticated stylistic technique: not only does each of its 22 stanzas begin with one of the successive letters of the Hebrew alphabet, but so does every verse in the stanza, and every verse contains at least one of the eight Hebrew words used to refer the law: *torah*, "law"; *dabar*, "word"; *'edût*, "testimony"; *mishpat*, "judgment"; *'imrah*, "commandment"; *hôq*, "statute"; *piqqudîm*, "precepts"; *miswah*, "ordinance." As if by a rosary wending its way from *alef* to *tau*, from A to Z, the believer must let himself be won over by this continuous prayerful thread, the longest of the whole Psalter, and must profess his joy at being ever with God, in all his hours and his choices in life. It is said that the philosopher Blaise Pascal recited this every day, while Dietrich Bonhoeffer, the theologian martyr of Nazism in 1945, wrote:

> Psalm 119 becomes especially difficult for us, perhaps, because of its length and monotony. In this case a rather slow, quiet, patient advance from word to word, from sentence to sentence, is helpful. Then we recognize that the apparent repetitions are always new variations on one theme, namely the love of God's word. As this love can never cease, so also the words which confess it can never cease. They want to accompany us through all of life, and they

become in their simplicity the prayer of the child, of the young man, and of the old man. (Bonhoeffer, op. cit., pp. 32–33)

—————

Psalm 122 (121): Jerusalem, city of peace

Here is one of the most impassioned songs of Zion and of the pilgrimage up to Jerusalem, a city set atop a mountain 800 meters high. In its first stanza (vv. 1–2) this lyric merges two distinct moments in time: the moment in the past in which the pilgrim decided to depart for the holy city, and the present moment in which his feet finally tread the earth in front of the city gates. Fascinated by the architectural and spiritual splendor of Jerusalem, the poet lets himself be won over by the desire to celebrate the city of his love, seat of the House of David and of the courts of appeal, the "thrones for judgment" which make for greater righteousness among the tribes of Israel (second stanza, vv. 3–5). The song ends with a final stanza (vv. 6–9) which is a "Franciscan" wish of "Peace and Good" for the beloved city. As often happens in the psalms of ascent to the Temple of Zion, this wish hints at the assonance between the word "Jerusalem," popularly interpreted as "city of peace," and the Hebrew word *shalôm*, "peace," with messianic contours.

—————

Psalm 128 (127): The song of the family

This delightful family picture — which has made the psalm one of the liturgical texts of Jewish and Christian marriage — sets upon the stage a father satisfied with his work, a wife full of life and fruitfulness like the vine, symbol par excellence of Israel blessed by God, children full of energy and vitality like the shoots of the olive tree, another tree dear to the Bible. An idyll of peace, serenity, happiness. But the door of the house seems to be open to Jerusalem: the little Jewish family is replaced by the great family of the nation upon which the same atmosphere of peace, serenity and happiness descends. This wisdom ode, which blossomed within a home, thus branches out into the liturgy of the Temple where the priests, blessing that family, see in it the sign of divine protection and of peace/*shalôm* (v. 6) over all of faithful Israel.

Psalm 130 (129): *De profundis*

The 52 Hebrew words of the *De profundis* have been repeated, translated and commented on more than those of many other psalms. And although it is often reduced to the rank of a funeral song, this supplication remains a splendid hymn to the joy of forgiveness. The cry of the worshiper rises from the abysmal places of evil hidden in the human heart, penetrates the heavens and leads from guilt to grace, from sin to redemption, from night to light. We would like to make just two observations on this page, so famous and so clear. The first concerns v. 4. For the psalmist, the fear of God arises not from judgment but from forgiveness, just as St. Paul suggests: "Do you presume on the riches of his kindness and forbearance and patience, not knowing that God's kindness is meant to lead you to repentance?" (Rom 2:4). The act of forgiveness must instill sorrow for the offended divine love; more than God's anger, it is His disarming love that must generate fear and sorrow. It is more bitter to strike a father than an implacable ruler. The second fact that we would like to underline is contained in the image in v. 6. The wait for forgiveness is the sigh of the whole being, just as sentinels spy the first threads of dawn light that mark the end of nocturnal fears. In the trepidation there is also the certainty that the sun will always rise with its bounty of light and life. But the word "sentinels" also more generically indicates "those who keep watch," perhaps also the priests who in the Temple await the day when they can preside — perhaps even just once in their lives due to their large number — over the worship of Israel. A holy and joyful waiting for God's love toward His creature.

Psalm 131 (130): A child in its mother's arms

The exquisite image that undergirds the few lines of this psalm of trust have made it one of the dearest to the Christian tradition. It is the song of a spontaneous and absolute, almost instinctive trust, similar precisely to the affectionate and serene clinging of the child to the person who constitutes its security and peace, that is, its mother. But this is not, as many think, the toddler still being breastfed; the Hebrew term used refers to the weaned child, so the image is the quite Oriental one of the child that the mother carries on her back. There is, therefore, a more conscious intimacy. Isaiah had already sung of the relationship between Israel and its God precisely on the basis of maternal symbolism: "Can a woman forget her nursing child, / that she should have no compassion on the son of her womb? / Even these may forget, / yet I will not forget you" (Is 49:15). In the finale the poet calls all of Israel to this intimacy, which is not understood by those whose hearts are swollen with pride and who aim for sensational successes: "O Israel, hope in the LORD, / from this time forth and forevermore" (v. 3).

―⁓⁓―

Psalm 137 (136): By the rivers of Babylon

Continuously taken up in the literary tradition down through all the ages, this powerful and dramatic lamentation of the Jewish exiles along the canals of Babylon after the destruction of Jerusalem in 586 BC must simply be left to the reader. There is no way to translate into a commentary its freight of desperation and hope, the sinewy power of its images, the dazzling intensity of its indignation and melancholy. The visceral love for Zion, the impossibility of desecrating the melodies of the Temple by singing and playing them in a foreign land, the brutality of the tormentors, the searing memories of the Edomites, vassals of Israel, who had collaborated with the Babylonians in razing the holy cities become material for sublime poetry. In the finale, the terrible curse against Edom and against Babylon, the devastator, remains on the lips: as you did to the Jewish children, so — according to the biblical justice of retaliation — may others dash your children to pieces on the rocks. A macabre scene, a sign of the "abasement" of the God of the Bible toward an oppressed humanity that has no weapon other than the word and the invocation of the just and avenging God. We explained the conception underlying this final curse when we dealt with the "imprecatory psalms."

〰️

Psalm 139 (138): Lord, you search me and know me

Here is another masterpiece of the Psalter, a hymn to the infinite, all-knowing, all-powerful God, a hymn of great power and sovereign beauty. The ode, belonging to the wisdom tradition, bears traces of passages from Jeremiah and Job: it was therefore composed in the post-exilic era (from the fifth century BC onwards). It is difficult in just a brief note to do justice to the many riches contained in these four stanzas dedicated to God's omniscience (vv. 1–6) and omnipresence (vv. 7–12), to the creation of man (vv. 13–18) and to the divine judgment on the wicked (vv. 19–24). Suffice it just to mention man's surprise at seeing that God already knows his utterance from the first word (v. 4); his vain escape from God in a mad flight into the heavens, into the underworld, toward the dawn and all the way to the farthest boundaries of the west (vv. 8–9); the darkness that becomes transparent to the gaze of God (vv. 11–12); the knitting of the fetus in the mother's womb, an embroidery of matchless beauty (vv. 13–15); the biography of every man already written by God in His book even before our days come to be (v. 16); the bitter indignation over the wicked who delude themselves that they can destroy the divine work (vv. 19–22). It is the song of the encounter between two mysteries, the infinite one of God and that of man, a "wonderful" creature (v. 14).

<hr />

Psalm 148: The alleluia of creation

A choral song of creatures led by the man who presides over this cosmic liturgy of praise, Psalm 148 is composed of two powerful *alleluias*. The first is the one that resonates in the heavens and has celestial singers (vv. 1–6). Their hymn is the celebration of creation and divine providence (vv. 5–6). The second *alleluia* is intoned by the earth, represented by an alphabet of creatures (22 created beings that constitute our earthly horizon) that celebrate the creative and redemptive action of God (vv. 13–14). All the inhabitants of heaven and earth are, therefore, called to the cosmic temple for a "symphonic" prayer to their one Lord, Creator and Savior.

Psalm 150: The final alleluia

The collection of Psalms closes with this choral *alleluia*. It is a lavish, solemn and musical song of praise to the Lord; it is the last message of the Psalter. A cascade of *alleluias* accompanies the Temple orchestra, which is here fully assembled in its entirety with the *shofar,* the "horn," the harp, the zither, the drums, the strings, the flute and the cymbals. But at the finale a supreme sound arises: it is the breath of every living being, which becomes prayer and praise (v. 6). This cosmic song, often transposed into music, closes the *tehillîm,* "praises," as the Jews named the Psalms.

Conclusion

———

Here ends our brief journey into the pages of the Psalter, which has become the book of Christian prayer par excellence, as attested by the Liturgy of the Hours, the responsorial psalms of the Liturgy of the Word and the many antiphons woven from psalmic texts. St. Ambrose, describing the resounding voices of the men, women and children singing the Psalms in his church in Milan, compared them to the "majestic swelling of the ocean waves." It is the great breath of humanity and creation that praise their Lord and Creator.

To wrap up this itinerary of ours, let's hear from a great master of Christian faith and theology, St. Thomas Aquinas, who considers the Psalter a synthesis of the biblical and theological message:

> It, in fact, embraces in its universality the material of all theology. The reason this is the biblical book most used in the Church is because it contains within itself all of Scripture. Its characteristic is that of repeating, in the form of praise, everything that the other books present according to the methods of narration, exhortation and discussion. Its aim is that of prompting prayer, of

elevating the soul to God through the contemplation of His infinite majesty, through meditation on eternal beatitude, through communion with the holiness of God and the active imitation of His perfection.

Available at
OSVCatholicBookstore.com
or wherever books are sold

In preparation for the Jubilee Year 2025, the Exploring Prayer series delves into the various dimensions of prayer in the Christian life. These brief, accessible books can help you learn to dialogue with God and rediscover the beauty of trusting in the Lord with humility and joy.

Prayer Today: A Challenge to Overcome
Notes on Prayer: Volume 1
by Angelo Comastri
In order to have saints, what is needed are people of authentic prayer, and authentic prayer is that which inflames with a fire of love. Only in this way is it possible to lift the world and bring it near to the heart of God. To pray in truth, we must present ourselves before God with the open wounds of our smallness and our sin. Only in this way will the encounter with God be an encounter of liberation and redemption.

Praying with the Psalms
Notes on Prayer: Volume 2
by Gianfranco Ravasi
This little guide to the Psalms includes four cardinal points: a general reflection on prayer, the breath of the soul; a panoramic look at the psalmic texts; a portrait of the two protagonists, God and the worshipper, but also the intrusion of the presence of evil; and finally, an anthology of brief commentaries on the Psalms most dear to tradition and the liturgy. The hope is that all the faithful may draw fully from this wonderful treasury of prayers.

The Jesus Prayer
Notes on Prayer: Volume 3
by Juan Lopez Vergara
This book explores the unique experience of the fatherhood of God for Jesus Christ, whom he calls Abba — which in his native Aramaic language means "Dad." Throughout his earthly life, Jesus is in contact dialogue with Abba. From his Baptism in the Jordan through his public ministry and ultimately his crucifixion, this relationship will mark him forever, transforming his life, and our lives, too.

Praying with Saints and Sinners
Notes on Prayer: Volume 4
by Paul Brendan Murray
The saints whose writings on prayer and meditation

are explored in this book are among the most celebrated in the great spiritual tradition. The aim of this book is to discover what help the great saints can offer those of us who desire to make progress in the life of prayer, but who find ourselves being constantly deflected from our purpose, our tentative efforts undermined perhaps most of all by human weakness.

Parables on Prayer

Notes on Prayer: Volume 5
by Anthony Pitta

What characterizes, in a singular way, Jesus's teaching on prayer is the recourse to parables. Jesus did not invent a new system for praying. Jesus was not a hermit, a Buddhist monk, or a yogi. He instead chose the daily life of his people to teach prayer with parables. This book explores the parables in the Gospels explicitly related to prayer. The reader is guided by Jesus, the original teacher of prayer with parables.

The Church in Prayer

Notes on Prayer: Volume 6
by Carthusian Monks

Carthusian Monks reside in several international monasteries. Founded in 1084 by Saint Bruno, the Order of Carthusians are dedicated to prayer, in silence, in community. Like other cloistered religious, the Carthusians live a life focused on prayer and contemplation.

The Prayer of Mary and the Saints
Notes on Prayer: Volume 7
by Catherine Aubin
When Mary appears, anywhere in the whole world, the places where she appears have points in common with the biblical places where she stayed and lived. This book reviews these places, examining what they reveal to us about Mary's identity, and what the inner spaces are that Mary asks us to dwell in today. This book also explores the unique relationship two holy women each had with Mary, leading us toward a new, deep revelation of Mary's closeness to each of us.

The Prayer Jesus Taught Us: The "Our Father"
Notes on Prayer: Volume 8
by Hugh Vanni
This book identifies the theological-biblical structure underlying the Lord's Prayer and situates it in the living environment of the early Church. This will give us a framework of reference, and as a result we will see first the antecedents in Mark, then the systematic presentation of Matthew, Paul's push forward, the accentuation of Luke, and, finally, the mature synthesis found in John.